Biomes of North America

A Walk in the Deciduous Forest

Rebecca L. Johnson

with illustrations by Phyllis V. Saroff

LERNER PUBLICATIONS / MINNEAPOLIS

*For my niece Claire, who helps me see
the world with fresh eyes*

—R. L. J.

Text copyright © 2001 by Rebecca L. Johnson
Illustrations copyright © 2001 by Phyllis V. Saroff

Map on page 8 by Laura Westlund © 2001 by Lerner Publishing
Group, Inc.

Lerner Publications Company
A division of Lerner Publishing Group, Inc.
241 First Avenue North
Minneapolis, Minnesota 55401 USA

For reading levels and more information,
look up this title at www.lernerbooks.com.

Library of Congress Cataloging-in-Publication Data

Johnson, Rebecca L.
  A walk in the deciduous forest / by Rebecca L. Johnson;
illustrations by Phyllis V. Saroff.
    p.   cm. — (Biomes of North America)
Includes index.
Summary: Takes readers on a walk through a forest of trees that lose
their leaves in the fall, showing examples of how the animals and
plants depend on each other and their environment to survive.
  ISBN-13: 978–1–57505–155–0 (lib. bdg. : alk. paper)
  ISBN-10: 1–57505–155–9 (lib. bdg. : alk. paper)
1. Forest ecology—Juvenile literature. 2. Forests and forestry—
Juvenile literature. [1. Forest ecology. 2. Forests and forestry.
3. Ecology.] I. Saroff, Phyllis V., ill. II. Title. III. Series: Johnson,
Rebecca L. Biomes of North America.
  QH541.5.F6 J63 2001
  577.3—dc21   00-008243

Manufactured in the United States of America
19-41702-4585-3/16/2016

Words to Know

amphibians *(am-FIH-bee-uhnz)*—frogs, salamanders, and other animals that begin life in water as tadpoles, but later grow legs and may live on land

biome *(BYE-ohm)*—a major community of living things that covers a large area, such as a grassland or a forest

bog *(bawg)*—a patch of spongy, soggy ground

climate *(KLYE-mut)*—a region's usual pattern of weather over a long period of time

deciduous *(dih-SIH-juh-wuhs)*—falling off. Deciduous plants lose their leaves at the end of the growing season.

hibernate *(HYE-bur-nate)*—to pass the winter in a special deep sleep

marsh—an area of wet, low-lying land near a pond or lake

predators *(PREH-duh-turz)*—animals that hunt and eat other animals

prey *(pray)*—animals that are hunted and eaten by other animals

talons—large, sharp claws

dancing in the breeze

A pileated woodpecker hops across the leaf-covered ground. He spies a plump acorn. But before the bird can grab it, a red fox leaps from the bushes. Feathers fly, but the woodpecker escapes. He soars to safety up in the treetops. His angry cries echo through the forest.

The woodpecker's home is a deciduous forest. It is a cool, shady place where tall trees grow. Nearly all the trees have broad, flat leaves. Their arching branches form a green roof high above the forest floor.

Leaves of deciduous trees come in many shapes and sizes.

red oak

silver maple

shagbark hickory

basswood

black walnut

Fallen maple leaves drift across the surface of a pond in a deciduous forest *(above right)*.

The word deciduous means "falling off." What falls off in this forest? Leaves do—billions of them. Most of the trees in a deciduous forest shed all their leaves each autumn. Every spring, new leaves grow.

Deciduous forests cover much of the eastern United States. They are also found in Europe and Asia. Imagine you are in a deciduous forest in an eastern state. You hike north. After several days, you see fewer deciduous trees and more evergreen trees. Evergreens keep their leaves year-round.

By the time you reach Canada, you're surrounded by evergreen trees. You're in the boreal forest. Keep traveling north, and you eventually reach a cold, treeless plain called the tundra.

Deciduous trees lose all their leaves every autumn. They grow new leaves every spring.

Biomes of North America

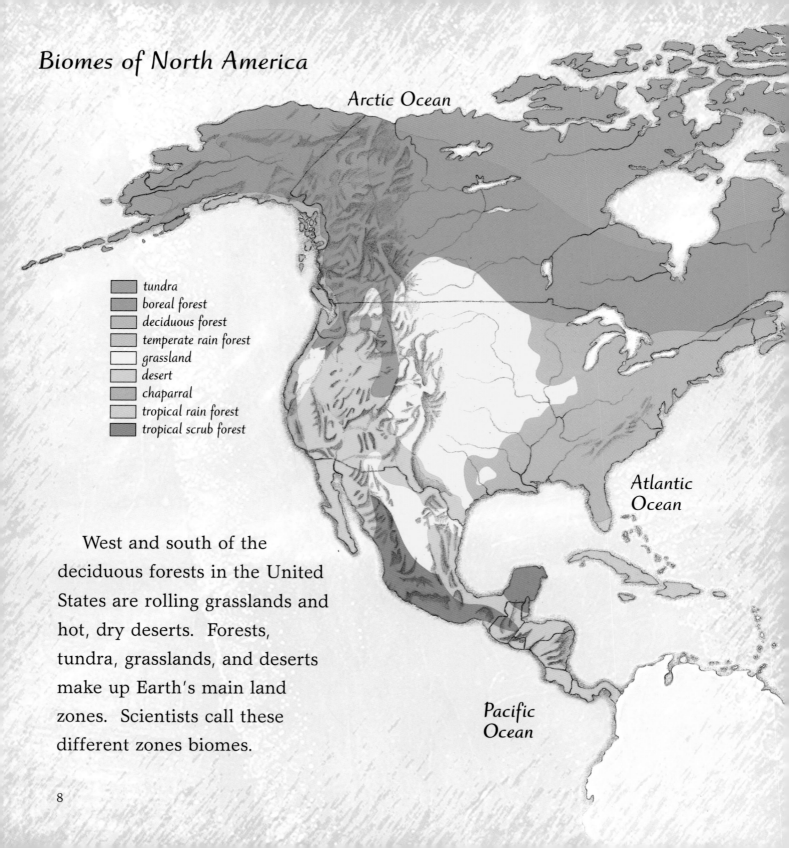

Arctic Ocean

■	tundra
■	boreal forest
■	deciduous forest
■	temperate rain forest
□	grassland
■	desert
■	chaparral
■	tropical rain forest
■	tropical scrub forest

Atlantic Ocean

Pacific Ocean

West and south of the deciduous forests in the United States are rolling grasslands and hot, dry deserts. Forests, tundra, grasslands, and deserts make up Earth's main land zones. Scientists call these different zones biomes.

Each biome has a different type of climate. The climate is an area's usual pattern of weather over a long period of time.

Every biome is home to a special group of plants. The plants are well suited to living in that climate and to growing in the soil found there.

In autumn, a deciduous forest is ablaze with color.

Every biome is also home to a special group of animals. In one way or another, the animals depend on the plants to survive. Many of a biome's animals eat plants. Other animals eat the plant-eaters.

Each spring, maple trees bloom. Then, new leaves grow from buds on the trees' branches. By early summer, maple leaves are large and green.

spring

summer

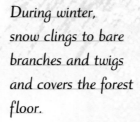

During winter, snow clings to bare branches and twigs and covers the forest floor.

All the plants and animals in a biome form a community. In that community, every living thing depends on other community members to survive. A biome's climate, soil, plants, and animals are all connected this way.

In general, deciduous forests have a moist, mild climate. But the weather changes quite a bit. There are four seasons: a warm rainy spring, a hot humid summer, a cool crisp autumn, and a cold snowy winter.

In winter, the leafless branches of the trees look like bony fingers reaching toward the sky. A few birds sing. Cold winds rattle the twigs. Mostly, the forest is silent beneath a soft blanket of snow.

In autumn, maple leaves turn orange, red, or gold. The leaves fall off, leaving the branches bare in winter.

autumn

winter

11

Trillium flowers bloom in spring, forming a carpet of white and green (above). The delicate blossoms of pink lady's slipper look like tiny pairs of shoes (right).

12

But when spring arrives, the forest comes to life in a sudden, spectacular rush. Gentle rains help melt the snow. Green shoots push up through the damp soil. Wildflower buds burst open. Purple violets, white trillium, and pink lady's slippers are some of the first flowers to bloom.

Bright green leaves sprout from the branches and twigs of deciduous trees.

A maple leaf uncurls in the warm, spring sunlight (above). *A flowering dogwood becomes a splash of white* (right).

The trees bloom, too. Most have very small flowers that you may not notice. But great numbers of seeds will come from those tiny flowers. Those seeds will be food for many forest animals.

All winter long, tiny new leaves have been safe inside buds. When the buds' scales open, the leaves unfold.

As the trees bloom, their leaf buds open. The hard coverings around the buds fall away. New leaves unfold in the sun's warm glow. The leaves use sunlight to make food that trees need to grow.

15

It is early summer. The spring flowers have faded, and the trees are leafy and green. Let's take a walk in the deciduous forest and see what life is like here.

Soft green light filters down through the treetops. The air is cool and damp. A thick layer of dead leaves covers the forest floor. Do you feel how soft and spongy it is under your feet?

Many different kinds of trees surround you. Broad-topped maples and hickories tower over you. The gnarled branches of oak trees twist toward the sky. The white bark of paper birches lights up the forest. Tall, stately elm, basswood, and walnut trees grow here, too.

Oak trees
are often the
tallest trees in a
deciduous forest.

Sunbeams flicker
through the treetops
to light up the slim,
graceful trunks of
the trees.

17

Young fern leaves are called "fiddleheads" because they look like the curled head of a violin.

Ferns and low-growing plants nestle at the base of a large, moss-covered trunk *(above right)*.

Small trees and bushes—hawthorn, dogwood, and holly—grow beneath the taller trees. Virginia creeper, wild grape, and bittersweet vines twine around the tree trunks. Lacy ferns and velvety mosses carpet the forest floor. Poison ivy grows here, too. So be careful what you touch.

Tiny creatures are busy on the forest floor. Some eat dead matter and turn it into soil. Others eat the soil-makers.

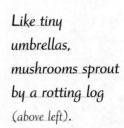

ant

centipede

snail

mite

pill bug

grub

Clumps of musty-smelling mushrooms sprout from fallen logs. Turn a log over. Worms, beetles, pill bugs, and millipedes run and wriggle for cover. These tiny creatures eat dead leaves, rotting logs, animal droppings, and the other dead plant and animal matter on the forest floor. They break the dead matter into smaller pieces, which become part of the rich, dark soil. The rich soil helps the plants become healthy and strong.

Like tiny umbrellas, mushrooms sprout by a rotting log (above left).

19

Just out of its cocoon, a new butterfly waits for its wings to unfold.

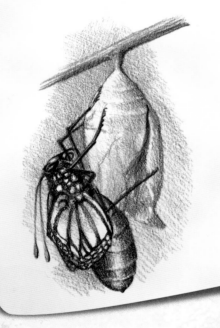

Caterpillars devour a poplar leaf (above right).

Look closely at the low-growing branch of that poplar tree. Something has chewed holes in the leaves. Caterpillars and other insects swarm over the tree, munching as they go.

Some caterpillars will soon change into butterflies and moths. They will flit through the forest on velvety wings.

Other winged creatures make their home here, too. Listen. *Wee-see, wee-see.* A black-and-white warbler whistles in the treetops. She is a summer

Hidden by a leafy branch, a warbler sits quietly on its nest (left). A prothonotary warbler (below) will usually build a nest in a hole in a tree trunk.

visitor to the forest. Every spring, warblers, vireos, flycatchers, and many other kinds of birds arrive from warmer places farther south. They join birds such as blue jays, woodpeckers, nuthatches, and chickadees that live here year-round.

A tidy nest holds the spotted eggs of a black-and-white warbler.

Chips of wood fly as a red-headed woodpecker hammers out a hole for its nest (above right).

All the birds are busy building nests and laying eggs. Woodpeckers hammer out new holes in tree trunks for their nests. Nuthatches and wrens build their nests in the holes that woodpeckers made last year or before. The black-and-white warbler you heard built her tiny nest near the bottom of a hickory tree. She's just laid three speckled eggs inside.

When their eggs hatch, mother and father birds work hard to gather food for hungry chicks. Warblers and flycatchers nab insects in midair. Nuthatches search for juicy bugs on tree trunks. Towhees scratch in the dirt for ants and worms. Woodpeckers drill into trees for beetles.

Woodpecker chicks peek out of their tree-hollow home, eager for food.

A downy woodpecker brings a juicy meal to its hungry chicks.

23

Some of the birds in the forest are predators.
Sparrow hawks chase smaller birds through the treetops.
When darkness falls, owls hunt on silent wings. They
are looking for smaller birds, mice, and voles.

Fluffy great horned owl chicks depend on their parents for food for many weeks.

A gray squirrel clings to the rough bark of a tree (left). A white-footed mouse nibbles on a seed (below).

Ferns rustle near you, and a cotton mouse steps into view. He sips dew from a leaf. The forest is full of mice, dormice, and woodland voles. These small rodents gnaw nuts and seeds with their strong teeth. They dig for worms and insects with their tiny paws.

Squirrels and chipmunks chatter in the treetops. They scurry up and down tree trunks. Like furry acrobats, they leap from branch to branch.

25

A weasel is thin enough to follow a mouse into its burrow.

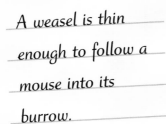

A pair of long ears twitches in the shadows. A mother rabbit is watching you. Somewhere close by, her babies are hidden. They lie quietly in their hiding place so weasels and minks won't notice them. These two forest predators are sleek and strong. With their slim, flexible bodies they easily slip into small spaces in search of a meal.

With its brownish gray fur, a cottontail rabbit is hard to see on the forest floor.

A snake sheds its old, outer layer of skin.

A breeze stirs something long and papery at your feet. It's a freshly shed snake's skin. Snakes shed the outer layer of their scaly skin from time to time as they grow. Green, hognose, and black snakes live in deciduous forests. They are harmless—except to the rodents and rabbits they hunt.

With every muscle tense, a long-tailed weasel watches its prey.

Frogs have suction cups on their toes. They can cling to slippery leaves and stems.

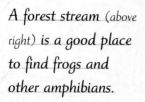

A forest stream (above right) is a good place to find frogs and other amphibians.

Up ahead, a stream gurgles over moss-covered rocks. On summer nights, frogs gather at the stream. Male frogs call to attract females. You can hear the high-pitched twangs of spring peepers and the low croaks of bullfrogs. Some frog calls sound like drumbeats. Other calls sound like someone burping!

A dark, shiny creature crawls out of the water. It's a salamander. Like frogs, salamanders are amphibians. They have smooth, slimy skin. They begin life as tiny, swimming tadpoles. As tadpoles, they eat tiny plants in the water.

As adults, most salamanders live on land. There, they look for worms and insects to eat. But because their skin dries out quickly, salamanders are never far from water.

Frog eggs don't have hard shells. Tadpoles grow inside a ball of clear jelly.

Salamanders have slimy, slippery skin.

29

Raccoons use their front paws to search muddy streambanks for frogs, worms, and crayfish (above). They often dunk their food into the water many times before eating it (below).

Young raccoons are good climbers. They love to go exploring.

Bend down and look carefully at the mud beside the stream. See that line of paw prints? Raccoons came here last night to drink. They also washed their food before they ate it. Raccoons eat everything from worms and frogs to berries and birds' eggs. During the day, they often hide in holes in trees.

Lying motionless on the forest floor, a spotted fawn is very hard to see.

Move deeper into the forest, where the ferns are waist-high. The silence is broken by a strange sound, like someone coughing. It's the snorting call of a white-tailed deer. She's warning her fawn that danger is near.

Owls fly silently because their feathers have soft, fluffy tips.

A great horned owl is perched in the treetops. With its razor-sharp talons outstretched, it could swoop down on a small fawn. Bobcats prowl the forest, too, especially at night. They look for deer, birds, rabbits, or anything else they can catch.

A great horned owl hunts rabbits, mice, and other small animals at night.

A fox crouches behind a tree trunk. It is waiting to pounce on the next mouse that wanders by. But foxes eat more than meat. You might also see a fox standing up on its hind legs, stripping juicy berries from a bush.

A young gray fox peeks out from the shelter of a bush.

Black bear cubs clamber through the treetops, looking for food. Bears are good climbers.

See the deep cuts in the bark of that large oak tree? A black bear sharpened its claws on the trunk. It needs sharp claws to dig and to climb trees. Black bears are the largest predators in the deciduous forest. They eat mice and squirrels and fish. But like foxes, bears also eat berries and nuts.

When frost nips the air, leaves of maples and other trees change color (right). *Dogwood berries* (below) *ripen in the autumn sun.*

The forest that surrounds you will soon change. As the summer months pass, seeds begin to ripen. Baby birds learn to fly. Young animals learn to survive on their own. The days get shorter, and summer gradually slips into autumn. After a few chilly autumn days, the forest changes color. Green leaves turn scarlet, yellow, orange, and gold. For a few weeks, the entire forest glows.

Geese paddle across a lake that reflects the bright colors of the autumn leaves.

Acorns are the seeds of oak trees. They begin as tiny flowers near the tips of branches.

Leaves flutter to the forest floor in a shower of yellow and gold.

But after two or three weeks, the beautiful leaves fall. Billions of leaves drift down from the treetops, tumbling and swirling in the wind. They settle on the forest floor and fade to brown and gray.

By autumn, acorns have grown into hard seeds with fuzzy caps.

Seeds fall along with the leaves. The winged seeds of maple trees spin to the ground like little helicopters. Acorns rain down from oaks. Walnuts land with thumps on the forest floor.

Cheek pouches stuffed with seeds, a chipmunk gets ready for winter.

Animals that spend the winter in the forest feast on these seeds and nuts. Woodchucks, dormice, raccoons, and bears eat and eat and eat, until they are round and fat. Squirrels and chipmunks store seeds in tree holes and beneath old stumps.

Most insects lay eggs and die. Some spin cocoons. There they will spend the winter. Other insects find shelter beneath loose bark.

In spring, oak tree seedlings may sprout from some buried acorns.

A plump raccoon stops for a drink (above left). Ladybug beetles cluster together to spend the winter under a fallen log (left).

Snakes hibernate together in an underground burrow.

Black-capped chickadees (above right) are year-round residents of the forest.

As winter approaches, most of the birds fly south to warmer places. Chickadees, nuthatches, and woodpeckers stay behind. They survive on stored seeds, tree buds, and berries. Some hunt for hidden insects.

Some forest animals hibernate. They curl up in dens or underground burrows and fall into a deep sleep. Most of them sleep until spring. Dormice hibernate in snug nests inside piles of leaves. Salamanders burrow into soft damp soil. Woodchucks hibernate in underground holes.

Raccoons, bears, and squirrels don't hibernate. But they do spend most of the winter snoozing in dens or caves or tree hollows.

When they're not sleeping, squirrels snack on stored nuts. On nice winter days, bears may leave their dens to look for food.

A sleepy black bear peers out of its den in the middle of winter.

Other forest animals simply endure the cold winter months. Deer find shelter from the wind and blowing snow. They feed on tender twigs, buds, and bark. Foxes, bobcats, and weasels hunt for rabbits and squirrels in the snow. They have thick coats of fur to keep them warm.

For several months, the forest lies hushed in a wintry sleep. But spring eventually returns. And when it does, the buds on the trees split open, new leaves unfold, and the deciduous forest comes to life again.

A hungry bobcat bounds through the snow after a snowshoe hare.

After a long, snowy winter, tiny flowers open along the branches of a red maple tree. New leaves will quickly follow.

for further
Information
about the
Deciduous Forest

Books

Arnold, Caroline. *Bobcats*. Minneapolis: Lerner, 1997.

Brown, Fern G. *Owls*. New York: Franklin Watts, 1991.

Fowler, Allan. *Raccoons*. Danbury, CT: Children's Press, 2000.

Fischer-Nagel, Heiderose and Andrea. *Life of the Ladybug*. Minneapolis: Carolrhoda, 1986.

Freeman, Marcia S. and Gail Saunders-Smith. *Black Bears*. Danbury, CT: Children's Press, 1999.

George, Jean Craighead. *One Day in the Woods*. New York: Harper, 1995.

Johnson, Sylvia A. *How Leaves Change*. Minneapolis: Lerner, 1986.

——. *Songbirds: The Language of Song*. Minneapolis: Carolrhoda, 2001.

Kalbacken, Joan. *White-tailed Deer*. Chicago: Children's Press, 1992.

Lepthien, Emilie U. *Squirrels*. Chicago: Children's Press, 1992.

Schnieper, Claudia. *On the Trail of the Fox*. Minneapolis: Carolrhoda, 1986.

Souza, D. M. *Frogs, Frogs, Everywhere*. Minneapolis: Carolrhoda, 1995.

——. *Slinky Snakes*. Minneapolis: Carolrhoda, 1992.

Stuart, Dee. *Bats: Mysterious Flyers of the Night*. Minneapolis: Carolrhoda, 1994.

Tresselt, Alvin. *The Gift of the Tree*. New York: Lothrop, 1992.

Winner, Cherie. *Salamanders*. Minneapolis: Carolrhoda, 1993.

——. *Woodpeckers*. Minneapolis: Carolrhoda, 2000.

Websites

Explore the Fantastic Forest
http://magma.nationalgeographic.com
/ngexplorer/0201/adventures

The National Geographic Society presents a game for children. Trek through a forest and learn about the wildlife there.

A Guide through the Northeastern Deciduous Forest
http://www.an.psu.edu/jxm57/trees
/slidepage.htm

This site provides pictures and information about many kinds of deciduous trees.

Temperate Deciduous Forest Biome
http://mbgnet.mobot.org/sets/temp
/index.htm

On this site from the Evergreen Project, you can learn about the temperate deciduous forest, its wildlife, and fall colors.

Photo Acknowledgments

The images in this book are used with the permission of: © Gary Braasch Photography, pp. 4–5, 6, 7, 9, 11, 12 (top left), 14 (left), 14–15, 16–17, 18, 19, 20, 21 (top), 29, 36 (top), 37, 38–39, 45; © Joel W. Rogers/ CORBIS, p. 5 (inset); © Richard Day/ Daybreak Imagery, pp. 12 (bottom left), 22, 23, 24, 30–31; © Frank Staub, pp. 12–13; © Gary W. Carter/CORBIS, p. 21 (bottom); Visuals Unlimited: (© Stephen J. Lang) p. 25 (top), (© William J. Weber) p. 25 (bottom), (© Gregg Otto) p. 26, (© Ron Spomer) p. 27, (© Bruce Clendenning) p. 28, (© Joe McDonald) pp. 30 (top), 30 (bottom), 44–45, (©W.A. Banaszewski) p. 32, (©R. Knolan Benfield, Jr.) p. 35, (© Gary W. Carter) p. 36 (bottom), (© John Gerlach) p. 40, (© Steve Maslowski) p. 41 (top), (© J. Alcock) p. 41 (bottom), (© Bill Banaszewski) p. 43; © Lydia Parker, p. 33; © Chase Swift/CORBIS, p. 34; © Tom Vezo, p. 42.

Front cover: © Rob and Ann Simpson/ Visuals Unlimited (woodpecker), © Gary W. Carter/Visuals Unlimited (deer), © Pat Anderson/Visuals Unlimited (trees).

Index

Numbers in **bold** refer to photos and drawings.